St. Murphy's Commandments

Ron Birk

LANGMARC PUBLISHING • SAN ANTONIO, TEXAS

St. Murphy's Commandments

By Ron Birk

Illustrator and Cover Artist: David Espurvoa
Cover Graphics: Michael Qualben

© Ron Birk, 1997

Published by LangMarc Publishing
P.O. Box 33817, San Antonio, TX 78265
Printed in the United States of America

Library of Congress Cataloging-in-Publication Data
Birk, Ron.
  St. Murphy's commandments / Ron Birk.
     p. cm.
  ISBN 1-880292-57-2
  1. Christian life--Humor. 2. Christian life--Caricatures and cartoons. 3. Church--Caricatures and cartoons.   I. Title.
BV4517.B47
230'.002'07--dc21

97-35613
CIP

Introduction

"If anything can go wrong—it will."

Of all the laws known to humankind, few are more famous than Murphy's classic observation. It contains just the right mix of truth and humor to make us smile and think at the same time.

Parkinson's Law, "Work expands so as to fill the time available for its completion," also has that unique characteristic. As does *The Peter Principle,* "In a hierarchy every employee tends to rise to his (or her) level of incompetence."

The popularity of such wry sayings has spawned countless other "laws," "codes," "theorems," "dictums," and the like. All are attempts to explain how our world really works. Not the way it *ought* to be, but the way it *is.*

St. Murphy's Commandments is a collection of observations about church life. A blend of wit and wisdom, of "Ha! Ha!" and "Ah-ha!," these sayings are meant to encourage as well as entertain those of us who know—and care about—our church.

Such "real rules of religion" gently remind us that the church is not always what it ought to be. The "communion of saints" is also the "communion of sinners," a *corpus permixtum* or "mixed bag," as Augustine noted. Therefore *The Pastor-Member Relationship Rule* advises us, "Don't be surprised when sinners act like sinners."

In spite of this ought/is gap, however, St. Murphy does not leave us in pessimistic despair. For there is *The Law of Hope:* "Even sinners sometimes do something saintly."

My hope is that you will enjoy and be entertained by Murphy's Commandments—perhaps even enlightened and encouraged.

But even if you are not, remember *The Grace Guarantee:* "You will be forgiven if you do and forgiven if you don't." —Ron Birk

The Termite Tenet:

Never underestimate
the importance of anything.

The Cool-It Concept: In an air-conditioned church, the number of men who are too warm will be equal to the number of women who are too cool.

The Primary Preaching Principle:

There is always a simpler,
clearer way to say it.

The Truth-in-Advertising Notion:
Beware of a preacher
named "Windy."

The Satan-is-Sly Precept:
Opportunity knocks;
temptation nudges.

Eve's Tenet of Temptation:
Each of us has
our forbidden fruit.

The It-All-Depends-on-How-You-Look-at-It-Directive:

A church looks different to a person standing in the pulpit looking one direction than it does to a person sitting in the pew looking the other direction.

The First Myth of Organized Religion:
Religion is organized.

The Law of Hope:

Even sinners sometimes
do something saintly.

The Hunger-for-Quiet Precept:
Stomachs growl only during silent prayers.

The Don't-Push Postulate:

The more obvious it is what
a pastor wants a congregation to do,
the less likely they are to do it.

The Dangers-of-Change Theorem:

The more a pastor works for change
in a congregation,
the more likely the congregation
will change pastors.

The Do-Unto-Others Dictum:

Parishioners listen to preachers
who listen to them.

The He-Who-Has-Ears-to-Hear-Has-Heard Law:
Experienced pastors are never surprised
by what they hear in counseling sessions.

The No Minimum Maxim:

When it comes to giving,
some members will stop at nothing.

The Balanced Budget Principle:
"Not-for-profit" organizations are also supposed
to be "not-for-loss" organizations.

The You-Can't-Please-'em-All Axiom:
When pastors try to please everyone,
they don't.

Corollary: No two members
have the same expectations of a pastor.

The Clothes-Don't-Make-the-Pastor Principle:
A colorful clerical shirt
doesn't always make a cleric colorful.

The Basic Rule of Church Communication:

Less is more.

Parkinson's Law, Bulletin Version:
Announcements expand
to fill the bulletin space available.

The Committed Committee Commandment:

Some of the best work in a church
is often done by a committee of three
—with two members absent.

The I-Move-We-Adjourn Axiom:

One of the major causes of church meetings
is church problems.

Corollary: One of the major causes
of church problems is church meetings.

The Birds-of-a-Feather Factor:

Any congregation that will accept you as a member also has other members who are sinners.

The Religious Reality Rule:
Even churches get roaches.

The Law of Congregational Expectation:

No one longs for a long sermon.

The Second Rule of Sermonizing:
If you can't preach that well,
don't preach that long.

The That's-the-Way-It-Is Rule:

There are Christian beliefs.
There are things Christians believe.
They are not always the same.

The Sticker Statute:
Good theology gets stuck in tiny libraries;
poor theology gets stuck on shiny bumpers.

The Mouth-Over-Mind Maxim:

The more closed the mind,
the more open the mouth.

The It's-Enough-to-Make-a-Grown-Person-Cry Maxim:
Babies in the cry room don't cry;
babies in the sanctuary do.

The If-the-Pew-Doesn't-Fit Principle:

No preacher is ever comfortable
in a pew.

The Too-Close-for-Comfort Commandment:

No parsonage
can be too far from the church.

The Rule of Emerging Emergencies:

Emergencies arise in direct proportion
to the fullness of a pastor's schedule.

The Axiom of Availability:
Church members really don't care
what pastors do with their time,
except that pastors must be readily available
whenever a member needs them.

The Statute of Limitations:

Never sign a three-year pledge
with a church that predicts the world
is coming to an end next week.

The Rule of Researching Religiously: Read enough theological books, and you will find someone who supports your belief.

Corollary: Have enough Bible translations in your library, and you will find one that agrees with what you think a particular passage says.

The Discipline Dictum:

Inside every short sermon there is a
long sermon struggling to get out.

The Law of Expecting the Unexpected:
Every sermon takes longer to preach
than the preacher thinks it will.

The Reaction Axiom:

For every pastoral action, there is a
congregational reaction.
The secret to pastoral success
is not to overreact to those reactions.

The Pastor-is-Always-the-Last-to-Know Theorem:
Pastors rarely know what's going on behind their backs.

The Disciples Dictum:

Twelve is not the limit.

The Too-Much-of-a-Good-Thing Theorem:

The more time spent in the church building,
the less time spent building the church.

The First Law of Liturgical Leadership:

If you can't chant,
—don't!

The Unexpected-Solo Rule:
There is an inverse relationship
between the choir director's favorite music
and the choir's ability to sing that music.

Parkinson's Law, Budget Version:

Expenses expand
to use all available income.

The Pledge-Is-Always-Greener Tenet:
Tithers always get a raise
when they move to another church.

The Code of Pastoral Success:

It's not who you please;
it's who you don't displease.

The Popularity Postulate:
Those who don't like the preacher
won't like the sermon.

The Grace Guarantee:

You will be forgiven if you do—
and forgiven if you don't.

The Forgiveness Factor:
Many want forgiveness.
Few want to forgive.

The Come-and-Go Theorem:

When a new pastor arrives,
17 percent of former inactive members
will become active,
while 17 percent of formerly active members
will become inactive.

The Watch-What-You-Say Commandment:

No one will remember everything a pastor says, but everything a pastor says will be remembered by someone.

Corollary: There will always be someone who remembers the pastor saying something the pastor never said.

The Congregation Communication Commandment:

Compliment publicly.
Complain privately.

The Airer-of-Your-Ways Warning:
Never make confession to a pastor
wearing a microphone.

The Ignorance-is-Bliss Precept:

There are members
who always *believe* what the Bible says,
even when they don't know *what* it says.

The Dogma Dictum: Let sleeping dogmas lie.

The More-Help-the-More-Work Principle:

The more people there are to help a pastor do the pastor's job, the more a pastor's job becomes helping those helping the pastor do the pastor's job.

The Dictum of Don't Do Too Much:
Pastors should never do
what a layperson can do.

St. Murphy's Commandment:

Anything a preacher says that can be misunderstood will be misunderstood.

The Law of Speaking Out: The surest way
for a pastor to find out how many members
are *against* an issue is to speak out *for* that issue.

The Grass-Is-Not-Always-Greener Rule:

Other churches' programs work
only in other churches.

The It's-Their-Fault Dictum:

When problems arise in the local church,
blame the church-at-large.

Corollary: When problems arise in
the church-at-large,
blame the local churches.

The Pastor's Phone Principle:

The voice you recognize
always identifies itself.
The one you don't never does.

The Over-Commitment Commandment:
Say "yes" enough and you will reach a point
where you wish you had said "no."

The Don't-Print-Them— And-They-Will-Come Code:

The fewer bulletins printed,
the more people
will attend worship that Sunday.

The Liturgical Octopus Principle:
Innovative worship experiences
usually require more bulletins and books
than any member can handle at one time.

The Occupational Hazard Principle:

The number of preachers listening to another
preacher preach is equal to the number
of listeners thinking,
"I could do better than that."

The Green Pastor's Postulate:
Every experienced pastor began
with no experience.

The Rule of Questionable Sermon Contents:

When in doubt,
throw it out!

The Think-or-Swim Maxim:
If you can't walk on water,
don't rock the boat.

The That's-Not-What-I-Heard Rule:

No two people
hear the same sermon.

The Time-Doesn't-Always-Change-Things Tenet:

Never change a church tradition
unless you know why
it became a tradition in the first place.

The Mustard Seed Maxim:

No problem is too small
to grow into a big problem.

The "Ooops!" Opinion:
Spilled communion wine
never falls on wine-colored clothes.

The Smarter-Is-Not-Always-Better Maxim:

Many pastors who complain
about their congregations
being theologically illiterate
would be out of a job if their members
were more theologically literate.

The Nobody-Said-It-Was-Easy Edict: The Gospel is simpler than most theologians make it out to be, but more complicated than most lay people think it to be.

The Gored-Ox Rule:

All church members
like sermons against sin
—unless it is *their* sin!

The Axiom of Overabundance:
Churches are donated the most
of what they need the least.

The Bishop-on-a-Hot-Tin-Roof Rule:

For a pastor,
nothing is worse than a nervous bishop,
especially when you are the one
making your bishop nervous.

The You-Can't-Win-for-Losing Law:
Pastors never win church arguments.

Parkinson's Law, Sunday Version:

Sunday school lessons expand
to fill the time allotted to them.

The Lay Reader's Rule,
or The Pocherethhazzebaim
Pronunciation Principle:

(see Nehemiah 7:59)

Read loudly, confidently, without pausing,
and listeners will accept your pronunciation;
hesitate, murmur, stammer, and they will wonder.

Corollary: There is no "proper" pronunciation
of Old Testament names.

The Principle of Honest Preaching:

Preachers never say everything
they *should* say to audiences
that pay their salaries.

The Rule of Interruptions: The closer to the pulpit
a child sits, the more likely she will get up
and go to the rest room during the sermon.

The Law of Grace:

There *is* a free lunch!

The Enjoy-It-When-It-Happens Edict:
No great spiritual moment is reproducible.

The Divorce Prevention Dictum:

Calling a pastor after one interview
is like proposing marriage after one date.

The Resumé Rule: All pastors look good on paper.

Corollary: All congregations look good
in their annual report.

The Pastor-Member Relationship Rule:

Don't be surprised
when sinners act like sinners.

The Pharisee Postulate:
Sins aren't sins
—if they are done by nice people like us.

The He-Who-Has-Ears-To-Hear Principle:

Good listeners
make good preachers.

The First Law on Sermon Comments:

Never tell a preacher
the sermon was too short.

The Don't Ask Dictum:

It is easier to get forgiveness
than permission.

The Let's-Face-the-Music Maxim:
Just because you donate the organ
doesn't mean you get to pick the organist.

The Judgment Judgment:

A pastor's good judgment
grows in direct proportion
to the number of bad judgments
a pastor makes.

The Sheep Pen Principle:
Shepherds always look
before they put their foot down.

The Church Building Code:

Churches without enough room grow;
churches with enough room shrink.

The Not-in-My-Back-Pew Dictum:
Visitors are always welcome
—unless they sit in my favorite pew.

The Law of Longevity:

Pastors leave.
Congregations stay.

The Age Gauge:
Young pastors want to save the world.
Old pastors want to save enough for retirement.

About the Author—

After twenty years as Lutheran Campus Pastor at Texas A&M and Southwest Texas State Universities, Ron Birk now divides his time between the Texas Hill Country ranch, which has been in his family for a century, and his career as a communicator.

As an actor, Ron has appeared in over two hundred commercial and industrial videos, as well as two movies. He is a popular humorous after-dinner speaker for associations, church and educational groups. "RONdom Thoughts," his column of humor and reflection, has appeared in Lutheran District and Synod newspapers since 1980. Collections of these columns have been published in two books: *What's a Nice God Like You Doing in a Place Like This?* and *You Can't Walk on Water If You Stay in the Boat.*

For speaking engagements, write to Ron Birk at—
101 W. Mimosa
San Marcos, Texas 78666
or call 512-396-0767.

About the Illustrator—

David Espurvoa is Director of Publishing Services at Texas Lutheran University in Seguin. He is a freelance illustrator and designer who graduated from Southwest Texas State University with a degree in Graphic Design and Illustration. He lives with his wife and their son.

To order *St. Murphy's Commandments*—

If unavailable at your local bookstore, call 1-800-864-1648. Your order will be shipped within 24 hours. Send $10.50 with your order to—LangMarc Publishing
P.O. 33817, San Antonio, TX 78265.